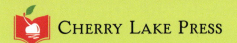

Published in the United States of America by Cherry Lake Publishing Group
Ann Arbor, Michigan
www.cherrylakepublishing.com

Reading Adviser: Beth Walker Gambro, MS, Ed., Reading Consultant, Yorkville, IL

Photo Credits: © wavebreakmedia/Shutterstock, cover; © Gorodenkoff/Shutterstock, 5; © Clovera/Shutterstock, 7; © Kilomeaters/Shutterstock, 8; © Mariusz Bugno/Shutterstock, 9; © Monkey Business Images/Shutterstock, 11; © loreanto/Shutterstock, 12; © PanuShot/Shutterstock, 13; © Summit Art Creations/Shutterstock, 14; © metamorworks/Shutterstock, 15; © Ian Dewar Photography/Shutterstock, 17; © SALMONNEGRO-STOCK/Shutterstock, 18; © Virrage Images/Shutterstock, 19; © Peopleimages.com-Yuri A/Shutterstock, 21; © Alexey Seafarer/Shutterstock, 22; © MAGNIFIER/Shutterstock, 23; © Monkey Business Images/Shutterstock, 24; © Quality Stock Arts/Shutterstock, 25; © Nikola Spasenoski/Shutterstock, 27; © 1st Footage/Shutterstock, 28; © Phoenixns/Shutterstock, 29; © Tapati Rinchmurus/Shutterstock, 31

Copyright © 2026 by Cherry Lake Publishing Group
All rights reserved. No part of this book may be reproduced or utilized in any form or by any means without written permission from the publisher.

Cherry Lake Press is an imprint of Cherry Lake Publishing Group.

Library of Congress Cataloging-in-Publication Data has been filed and is available at catalog.loc.gov.

Cherry Lake Publishing Group would like to acknowledge the work of the Partnership for 21st Century Learning, a Network of Battelle for Kids. Please visit Battelle for Kids online for more information.

Printed in the United States of America

Note from publisher: Websites change regularly, and their future contents are outside of our control.
Supervise children when conducting any recommended online searches for extended learning opportunities.

Diane Lindsey Reeves likes to write books that help students figure out what they want to be when they grow up. She mostly lives in Washington, D.C., but spends as much time as she can in North Carolina and South Carolina with her grandkids.

CONTENTS

Introduction:
In the Know | 4

Chapter 1:
**Logistics Managers Know...
How to Move Things Along | 6**

Chapter 2:
**Logistics Managers Know...
All About Logistics | 10**

Chapter 3:
**Logistics Managers Know...
The Tools of the Trade | 16**

Chapter 4:
**Logistics Managers Know...
How to Work Safely | 20**

Chapter 5:
**Logistics Managers Know...
How to Find the Job They Want | 26**

Stop, Think, and Write | 30
Things to Do If You Want to Be a Logistics Manager | 30
Learn More | 31
Glossary, Index | 32

In the Know

Every career you can imagine has one thing in common: It takes an expert. Career experts need to know more about how to do a specific job than other people do. That's how everyone from plumbers to rocket scientists gets their job done.

Sometimes it takes years of college study to learn what they need to know. Other times, people learn by working alongside someone who is already a career expert. No matter how they learn, it takes a career expert to do any job well.

Take **logistics** managers, for instance. They are responsible for moving goods from places where they are made to places where they are sold. Food, clothing, technology, automobiles—they all make exciting journeys before you can buy them.

Look around the next time you visit a superstore like Target or Walmart. All those products came from places all over the world. Many of them have traveled more than you have! And it's all because logistics managers made it happen.

Logistics managers are good at:

- Keeping track of lots of details
- Analyzing data from multiple sources
- Communicating with people from all over the world
- Problem-solving and critical thinking
- Using technology and special **supply chain** software

CHAPTER 1

Logistics Managers Know...How to Move Things Along

People all over the world love to wear blue jeans. But did you know that most jeans are made in Asia? Someone has to make sure people everywhere can buy them in stores. The professionals who make this happen are logistics managers.

Jeans are just one example. Imagine every product in every store in every country in the world. That will give you an idea of the gigantic task that logistics managers have. Their job is to get all those products to the places and people who need and want them.

Logistics is part of the global supply chain. A supply chain includes all the people and companies involved in creating a product and delivering it to **consumers**. This process takes a product from start to finish.

Clothing is a huge part of the global supply chain. Millions of clothing packages are shipped every day.

Cotton takes over 150 days to grow. There are thousands of cotton farms in the United States, many of which provide the material used to make our clothes.

In the case of blue jeans, it starts in the fields where cotton is grown. Logistics managers work to move raw materials like cotton, indigo dye, and copper to clothing factories. The copper is for rivets on the jeans.

This can be a mind-boggling task. Cotton must be processed and transported from fields in Brazil or India. It then has to get to factories in China. Copper used to make rivets for jeans is mined from rocks found in Chile,

the United States, and Peru. **Synthetic** indigo dye, zippers, and thread must be sourced and shipped as well. It takes a worldwide tour to make a simple pair of jeans!

Logistics managers help figure out where to get supplies. They find out how much **inventory** is needed. They look for the quickest and most cost-effective ways to move products. Everything is on a tight timeline. It takes lots of organization and strong problem-solving skills to get the job done.

WORLD-CLASS CHARLESTON HARBOR

Charleston, South Carolina, is home to one of the busiest **shipping ports** in the world. Every year, more than 4 million huge containers move from cargo ships to shore. Then they move onto trucks and trains heading for destinations near and far. Everything from automobiles and food to paper and plastics comes in and out of this port. The port is a huge employer. It accounts for one in nine jobs in South Carolina.

CHAPTER 2

Logistics Managers Know...All About Logistics

Logistics managers are supply chain experts. They must have a solid understanding of all the steps involved in getting products and supplies from point A to point B. In many ways, it's like putting together a huge puzzle. Each piece must fit perfectly in its place to keep the process moving.

The number one skill logistics managers need is problem-solving. They need the ability to think clearly and act quickly under pressure. Imagine a cargo ship containing millions of dollars' worth of products. Now imagine it has to change course to avoid a huge storm. How will the delay affect the rest of the supply chain? Can the trucks and dock workers be rescheduled for the new arrival time?

Logistics managers collaborate to solve problems. They work in teams.

It is important that logistics managers don't lose people's belongings. From packaging to shipment, organization is critical.

Is there a way to make up lost time? Or imagine Company X, at one end of the world, needs a huge supply of buttons. This may be for a rush order of men's shirts. Then—oops!—Company Z sent the buttons to the wrong destination. The pressure is on to get things back on track. The logistics manager needs to ensure Company X doesn't lose an important business deal.

Logistics managers need to have good people skills. They need to be able to talk and negotiate with others.

Logistics covers several big areas. A logistics manager may not be responsible for all of them. But they do need to understand how they all fit together. Logistics managers know that companies and **consumers** rely on them to manage the supply chain. Supply chains get everything from medicine to makeup where it needs to go.

ROBOTS WORK SMARTER, NOT HARDER

Robots are often used on docks and in warehouses. They take on the manual labor of loading and unloading products from delivery trucks or shipping containers. As is often the case, robots do jobs that are difficult or unpleasant for humans to do. They also help process customer orders in warehouses. They help reduce human foot traffic and speed up delivery processes. If you ever wonder how big warehouses can process orders so quickly, think "robots."

Warehouse workers use scanning technology to keep track of products. This helps them count their inventory.

Opportunities abound in five key areas:

1. Planning and information management
2. Product packaging
3. Transportation management
4. Storage, warehousing, and materials handling
5. Inventory management

CHAPTER 3

Logistics Managers Know...The Tools of the Trade

The steady supply of products around the world depends on a reliable transportation system. Logistics managers figure out the best way to transport each product. Cargo ships, trains, trucks, and aircraft are all options. Each comes with its own set of pros and cons. How long will it take? What will it cost? How many containers are needed? There are many questions to answer to make the best plan.

Logistics managers rely on all kinds of technology to do their jobs. They use special software to keep track of supplies and schedules. They use it to plan international transportation schedules. They use it to analyze inventory and other data. Having information available at their fingertips helps logistics managers stay organized.

Hundreds of trains travel across the United States every day. Many of them carry important supplies and products to new locations.

LOGISTICS GOES BANANAS

Bananas are the world's fourth largest crop. They are grown in tropical locations in Central America, Asia, and Africa. But what if you live in Miami, Florida, and you want to buy some?

A major banana plantation is located in Costa Rica. Bananas are harvested, packaged, and loaded into refrigerated containers on a big cargo ship. The ship goes through the Caribbean Sea and the Gulf of Mexico. It docks at the Miami Port on the Biscayne Bay. The trip is 1,120 miles (1,802.5 kilometers) long. It takes about 2 ½ days.

At the port, a big crane lifts the container from the ship. It then loads it onto the back of a truck. The truck stops by a warehouse for the container to be unpacked. The warehouse workers sort the bananas. Then the bananas are on another truck to a grocery store.

If kept cool, bananas will last 2 ½ weeks from farm to store. There is no time to waste before getting them on the produce shelf! That's where you find your favorite fruit to buy.

Many products are transported in cargo containers. These huge metal shipping boxes must be packed carefully. This is so that products are not damaged during transport. It can be quite a task figuring out how much to ship in each container. The good news is there is software for that.

When cargo ships come into port, they have to be unloaded. Ship-to-shore cranes do the heavy lifting. A ship can contain as many as 10,000 cargo containers and can take 1 to 3 days to unload. Special tracking devices help logistics managers keep track of what each container holds and where it needs to go.

Fleets of trucks and railroad cars are ready to take cargo from ports to warehouses. This is where the products are distributed to all the places that will use or sell them. Warehouse workers use forklifts and robots to move products from one place to another.

CHAPTER 4

Logistics Managers Know...How to Work Safely

In many cases, logistics managers handle safety concerns. There are so many moving pieces involved in the supply chain process. There are people, products, lots of equipment, and many vehicles. Safety is a big concern.

In fact, safety is so important in logistics that many jobs they work with are built around it. Safety trainers teach other employees how to do their jobs safely. Safety inspectors check vehicles, equipment, and facilities to make sure they meet safety standards. The Occupational Safety and Health Administration (OSHA) makes lots of rules that companies must follow to keep things safe for employees.

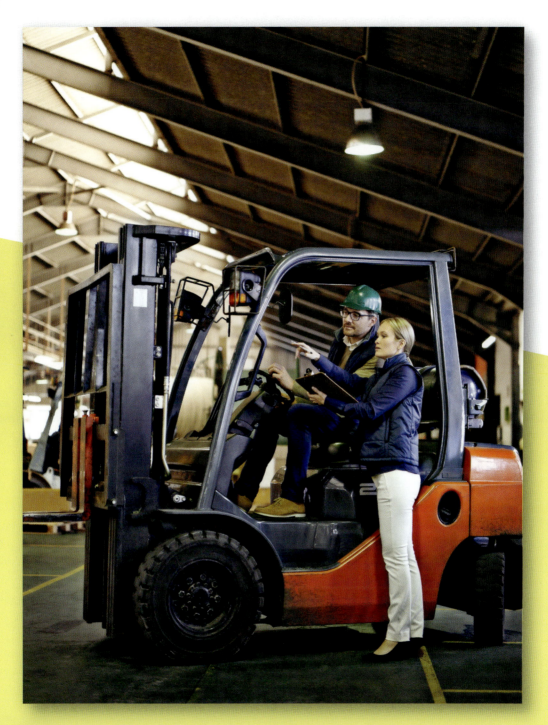

Workers take safety precautions when handling large machines. They may wear goggles and helmets for protection.

Every person on a cargo ship is highly trained. Experienced captains steer the ships over long distances.

Just think about what it takes to keep a fleet of cargo ships safe. The ships are filled with thousands of huge containers that must be loaded correctly. Each ship's mechanical system must be kept in top shape so the ship doesn't break down when out to sea. Living conditions for the crew must be sanitary and somewhat comfortable. Ships must be able to accommodate long voyages.

Now multiply all that times all the different types of vehicles used in logistics. There are fleets of trucks and truck drivers to take care of. Plus airplanes and pilots with different types of safety needs. Thousands of miles of railroad tracks that must be maintained to keep trains running safely.

Many of the products need special care. Some need refrigerated containers to avoid spoiling. Precautions must be taken when transporting chemicals and other combustible products.

A LOGISTICS RIDDLE

What equipment used in logistics is named after a bird, was modeled after human hands, and helps build itself?

Answer: Container cranes! These huge industrial machines are made in the likeness of birds called cranes. The birds have heavyset lower bodies and long, flexible necks and heads. Human hands inspired how crane machines operate. They move things efficiently and even mimic the way human knuckles bend. The only thing big enough and strong enough to build a crane is another crane. Workers use them to assemble new cranes.

Every person in a warehouse has an important role, whether it's tracking inventory or supervising others.

At large ports, workers use walkie talkies to communicate with others, give directions, and make sure everything is going safely and smoothly.

Bustling ports are like beehives of activity. Ships are docking. Cranes are lifting container after container off ships. Trucks are constantly coming and going. Many rules are in place to keep the process orderly.

Then there are the warehouses. Aisle after aisle is stacked floor to ceiling with all kinds of products. People can get hurt if products are not handled correctly and stored properly. Employees are trained in the best ways to lift and carry products. They must wear protective clothing.

Keeping all the fast-moving parts going in the right direction is the goal of all logistic safety efforts. It is something that affects every job along the supply chain.

CHAPTER 5

Logistics Managers Know...How to Find the Job They Want

As you now know, there are five main parts to the supply chain process. Information and control play a big role. So does transportation. Packaging all those products for transport and sale is another part. Inventory involves keeping track of what's what and where it's at. Then there is storing the products in warehouses and handling them for distribution. Each part of the process offers plenty of career opportunities.

Many careers are available for people who like to be in charge of all these areas. Supply chain managers move goods from suppliers to customers. They make transportation plans. They find companies to provide logistics services. They manage warehouses and distribution centers. Part of their job is to make sure shipments stay on time and on budget.

Logistics managers are trained by others with more experience. They observe experts to get better at their jobs.

Operations managers handle tasks like hiring and training employees. They also make budgets. They predict how much of a product is likely to sell. They may also help secure raw materials. This type of career is especially good for someone with a background in business management or accounting.

Logistics engineers are all about finding ways to make the process better, faster, and less costly. Demand planners use research and data analysis to predict how much of a product the market needs.

Warehouse managers are in charge of the huge facilities where products are stored. They oversee warehouse staff who process orders. Think of Amazon to get a sense of how big this job can be.

HELP WANTED

Business is booming for logistics! In fact, job opportunities in this field are expected to grow by a whopping 19 percent over the next **decade**. This is much faster than expected for other occupations. This is good news if you want a career getting the world's stuff where it needs to go.

Fleet managers work with truck drivers to make sure they are following the rules. They also plan their routes in advance.

Fleet managers manage the trucks used to move products from one place to another. They work with dispatchers and truck drivers. Fleet managers plan driving routes and communicate with drivers. They also make sure that safety rules are followed. Keeping vehicles in good repair is an important part of the job.

Inventory managers keep track of products. They record deliveries, check ships, and inspect stock.

Activity

Stop, Think, and Write

Can you imagine a world without logistics managers? How do they make the places we live, work, and play better?

Get a separate sheet of paper. On one side, answer this question:

- *Where in the world do some of the products you like to use come from?*

On the other side of the paper:

- *Draw a map showing the journey of your favorite food from where it gets made to where it gets sold.*

Things to Do If You Want to Be a Logistics Manager

It is likely that this is the first time you've heard about a logistics manager. Now that you know how interesting this career is, you may want to consider it for your future. What can you do to prepare for a career in logistics?

NOW

- Practice organizing systems for things like your family's food pantry, your closet, or your books.
- Take every opportunity you can to travel by car, train, plane, and boat.
- Think about if you'd rather work in the transportation, distribution, or inventory side of the supply chain.

LATER

- Look for volunteer or internship opportunities to get firsthand experience.
- Complete professional certification in supply chain management or logistics.
- Earn a college degree in supply chain management.

Learn More

Books

Meyer, Megan Preston. *Supply Jane and Fifo Fix the Flow.* Philadelphia, PA: Preston Meyer Publishing, 2023.

Newland, Sonya. *Working with Transport.* Tulsa, OK: Kane Miller, 2022.

Schmitt, Kelly Rice. *I Ship: A Cargo Ship's Colossal Journey.* Minneapolis, MN: Lerner, 2023.

On the Web

With an adult, learn more online with these suggested searches.

Defense Logistics Agency — What is the Defense Logistics Agency? — Video for Kids

Kiddle — Logistics Facts for Kids

PBS — GPS for Success — Transportation, Distribution, and Logistics

Glossary

consumers (kuhn-SOO-muhrz) people who purchase goods and services for personal or business use

decade (DEH-kayd) period of 10 years

fleets (FLEETZ) group of vehicles, ships, or aircraft owned by the same company

inventory (IN-vuhn-tor-ee) how many materials, goods, or products a business has available; the process of tracking those items

logistics (luh-JIH-stiks) use of people and computers to figure out the best and quickest way to move products from one place to another

rivets (RIH-vuhts) small pieces of metal used to reinforce pockets on jeans

shipping ports (SHIH-ping PORTS) seaside facilities with one or more wharves or loading areas where ships load and unload cargo and passengers

supply chain (suh-PLIYE CHAYN) all the processes involved in making and distributing a product to customers

synthetic (sin-THEH-tik) products made from artificial substances that mimic a natural product

Index

activities, 30

bananas, 18

cargo containers, 9, 18–19, 22–23, 25
Charleston, South Carolina, 9
clothing, 4, 6–8, 12
communication skills, 5, 10, 13, 29
cotton, 8
cranes, 19, 23, 25

fleet managers, 29
food shipping, 4, 9, 18, 23, 30

inventory tasks, 9, 14–16, 24, 26, 28–29

job market, 26, 28

logistics engineers, 28
logistics managers
   job descriptions, 4, 6, 9–20, 22–29
   skills, 5, 9–10, 13–14, 30
   tools, 5, 14–19, 22–23, 25

manufacturing sources, 6, 8–9
materials handling, 14–15, 19, 21, 24, 26

operations managers, 28

plane transportation, 15–16, 23
planning, 15–16, 26, 28
problem-solving, 5, 9–12, 16

robots, 14–15, 19

safety, 20–26, 29
shipping and ports, 9–10, 15–16, 18, 22, 25
shipping containers, 9, 18–19, 22–23, 25
superstores, 4, 28
supply chains, 4, 6, 9–10, 14–16, 20, 25–26

training, 20, 27–28, 30
train transportation, 9, 15, 17, 19, 23
transportation of goods, 4, 6, 9–10, 15–19, 22–23, 26, 29
truck transportation, 9, 15–16, 18–19, 23, 25, 29

warehouse processes, 14–15, 19, 21, 24, 26, 28

32